GOD OUT

GOD OUTSIDE THE CHURCH

J. W. STEVENSON

THE SAINT ANDREW PRESS

Published in 1972 by
The Saint Andrew Press
121 George Street, Edinburgh EH2 4YN

ISBN 0 7152 0211 1

Printed in Great Britain by Howie & Seath Ltd., Edinburgh

Contents

1 · So many beliefs—does it matter?

Four hundred people sitting in a church. The building says Belief. The Bibles in the pews say Belief. The service says Belief—in a presence, in a power, in 'effectual prayer'. But what do the people sitting there really believe? If their secret hearts were laid bare what would be revealed? Some belief, some uncertainty, some doubt, a lot of groping?

Yet we go on saying 'Church' as if, by and large, we are one company, with the same beliefs. Does it matter?

Every congregation is a mixed company. There will be some with assured belief. They speak 'the things which they have seen and heard'. They accept the basic truths of the Scriptures, the teaching and the worship of the Church.

There will be many—perhaps a great many—who have 'faith' in a less explicit sense, even though they have taken their vows. They find in Jesus a meaning, a depth, for their assessment of human life, whatever words they would put to it. They feel it right to be in the Church which bears His name; but they find some of the doctrine difficult to understand; much of it seems elaborate intellectual argument and they are not competent to enter into it. Some have doubts about parts

1

of the Bible but do not know how important these parts are. Some are drawn by sheer rebellion against a world which has gone so far wrong with its values, its ideas of power, its objectives in 'security', its standards of the desirable life—they turn to the life and teaching of Jesus as to something clean and pure, wholesome and purposeful, in a confused world. Their beliefs vary enormously—what they accept, what they hold on to and what they set aside.

And of course there are those with other kinds of reasons for being there: people who wish to keep some of the practices of the faith in which they have been brought up; the husband there because his wife wants to go, the father and mother there 'for the sake of the children', the people in public positions who see the support of the Church as part of their duty.

A great mixture of belief—does it matter?

However vague the belief and the motive, are these people there because they have been baptised into the Church to which the Spirit has been given, and in that sense received the Spirit —even if they have little understanding that the Spirit has given them the motive to come?

But there must surely be another kind of receiving of the Spirit if the Gospel is true, receiving what the New Testament calls the 'power of the Spirit'. What does that mean—what difference does it make?

Are the people who are there on the fringe of belief only a problem, a handicap, giving a false 'image' of the Church—or are they one clue to the meaning of the Church, being there at all—but only one clue?

What we are trying to do in the following pages is to find out what are the distinguishing marks of the work of the Spirit abroad in men and embodied in the Church, and what are the unique marks of the work of the Spirit received 'in power', recognisably turning men (as Paul says) from darkness to light, 'from the power of Satan to God', opening up for us the new life in Christ 'in the power of his resurrection'.

Is the Church only for those who have come into this faith— or is it also for the seekers who are learning the signs in themselves and other people which make them hold to some sort of belief about human nature and make many of them look to Jesus for the ultimate in human life? And how are all these people at different levels of belief to be held together?

A lot of the confusion about the Church begins here. We proclaim what it ought to be doing, what it is failing to do, what its mission to the world is, what it is to say and do about the dominant life-shaping social pressures of our time. We want to think of the Church as the whole people of God, not just as ministers, courts and assemblies, the 'establishment'; but we find ourselves implying that this 'whole people' can be expected to be doing the same things, to be capable, whatever the level of their faith, to speak in the name of Jesus, to 'witness', to 'bear testimony' that the life which they now live they live 'by the power of the Son of God'.

How much consensus of belief is there? We do not know. Ministers have to preach to these people as if to one body. Ministers have to exhort them to 'support the Church' as if they were one body. The Church calls upon them to go out on mission to the 'outsider' with the Gospel, as if they were one body.

How can we deal with this, when it is not known what this 'whole people' really believe, and yet are gathered together in one place marked 'Belief'—with pressures upon them from the attitudes to which they are habituated by their work, pressures from the popular thinking of the day, pressures from things done and known to be wrong and yet built in as necessities of circumstance? Only by recognising that some particular work of the Spirit brings us together, some particular action of the love of God, related to our condition, our judgments on right and wrong, our assessments of other people, our build-up and breakdown of relationships. This is the work of the Spirit, this particularity of the love of God in people at the humblest levels—and we have to learn the signs of it together.

The very make-up of the congregation then becomes prophetic for the Church's mission to the world. The world is with us in the shape of belief and unbelief within our church walls.

But how can we be helped by the Scriptures to distinguish between different 'areas' of the Spirit's action? There is one answer, at least the first part of it: to be taken back into the 'school of Christ' in an obscure Roman province, Galatia, to find the apostle Paul dealing with a similar situation. He said we have to be brought back to the essentials if we are to expect to be one body. After that—only after that—can we expect to learn what the Spirit is doing at other levels and to be 'workers together with God' in it.

The young Christian congregations in Galatia were perplexed. It may have been here that for the first time Christians had to ask themselves how much they were to take from the civilised, cultured community of which they were part; in fact, how much of the new knowledge about human nature and human society was of God, even if it was not 'Gospel'. Was God at work in men in different ways and at different levels? Was the creator Spirit troubling, urging, correcting, enlightening all of them, even if they were not ready or willing to receive him as Holy Spirit, opening their eyes to a new dimension of living?

There was the 'light which lighteth every man coming into

the world'. The signs of it were there to be seen in people who did not call themselves Christian. Christians had to discern it. Yet this was clearly not all that had been revealed in the coming of the Spirit 'in power': the 'fullness' of God, the miraculous gift of grace which had been given through Jesus Christ. How was the one to be related to the other?

Galatia had been for centuries one of the Celtic lands. Later the Celtic Church became distinctive for its faith that the Gospel was for the whole of life, the whole of society; for politics, for trade, for the ordering of the whole world of men.

These small Christian communities in Galatia were in a predicament, perhaps for this reason. Christians could not escape the pressure to fit the Gospel into this exciting new world they were living in, with its stimulus to fresh thinking, new experiments and radical assessment of the potentialities of human society. Much of this seemed to the young Christian Church to be of God—the imagination, the zest for knowledge, the search for meaning in what was 'human'. But many began to be confused between this and what the Gospel said about the 'world'.

How did you repent of, and yet learn from, this life in the world of which you were part? How did you receive 'grace' to live a new life and yet go on doing what your daily work compelled you to do? How did you receive the Holy Spirit but continue to order your life as an ordinary citizen in the community, with its social institutions, its accepted philosophy, even if shot through with insights revealing a work of God?

Some were being lured away from the Gospel—the more rigid Jewish Christians saw it like that. They had to be brought back to the observance of the Law, which had not been superseded, and the personal and public ritual which held it together—it was there still to give them certainty and discipline and a clear obedience to perform.

Paul saw that this was what we would call today counter-productive. It created the very attitude it was meant to correct. It was not just a recall to the faith of the Gospel. It was retreat into security, where the risks of involvement in the life of the community were eliminated—but so also were the 'risks' of faith.

What was being denied by these narrow Jewish Christians was that very 'grace' which was the heart of the Gospel—the supernatural work of God in Christ through the Holy Spirit. They were concentrating men's thoughts on what *they* were to do to keep right with God, how *they* were to achieve what God required of them, how *they* were to justify themselves in his sight and fulfil his demands.

This was back into the bondage of the Law. This was humanism trying to answer humanism, as if man could save himself by his own obedience.

In that form it is not our predicament. But in a new form we are where they were, convinced that we have much to learn from the science of our day, sure that God is at work in the compassion, the caring, the search for deeper truth about the human personality and personal relationships, and the quest for a society which encourages this kind of human development —and yet, along with this, confused whether this is all that the Spirit of God is.

We are under pressure to jettison whatever in the Gospel does not seem to fit into the categories of the new knowledge: supernatural grace; the miracle of restored relationship to God in Christ's atonement; the new dimensions of the life of faith; prayer in the power of the Spirit; the kingdom of heaven.

There is with us too the reaction from those who, because of this, are afraid for the Gospel and the Church and recall us to what has given a secure basis for the Christian life in the past: the forms of worship, the guidance which gave the Christian clear instruction what to do to keep himself within the practice of the faith, to fulfil what the Lord required of him, to observe what had been laid down in Scripture, to be meticulous in obedience to what had been established as right conduct.

We are not being lured back into a bondage to the Old Testament Law; but there are other kinds of bondage; sometimes it is to the tradition of the Church, to the structure of the institutions which have served us well, to a loyalty to what has held the Church together; sometimes just to the maintenance of what has been proved to be good in keeping Christian principles and ideals before the community.

How much of this reaction comes from fear, from defensiveness, just when boldness is required? How much of it results in emphasis on what *we* are to do to meet the temptations of our day, what is required of us, what our effort must be, what our duty is? One kind of humanism produced to counteract another? The Gospel of the grace of God can be eliminated in different ways in the very process of trying to secure it against the inroads of the agnostics.

Paul's drastic words to the young Christian communities in Galatia were for those who were drawing the Church into this subtle humanism. His letter became Scripture because it was about a fundamental 'double-think' which would always assail the Christian Church—the wrong answer to the overcoming of the world, the retreat from the Gospel in order to save the Gospel, the twist which results first in concentrating men's efforts on what they are to do to save 'Zion' and then in the erosion of the supernatural grace without which the Gospel ceases to be Gospel.

So this is still Scripture for us—unlikely as Galatia of the first century is as a place to look for it; and very different as the issues seem about which Paul wrote. How do we receive the Spirit?

The belief that the Holy Spirit is given for the whole life of men, and given in the very processes of the day's living implies that we must be concerned as Christians for the whole world of man's life, for the objectives society sets before itself, for every insight into the human personality and into the methods and motivation of men living and working together. This was what the Galatian Christians were groping after: a Gospel which was to overcome the world and claim the whole of man's life for Christ. 'It is not yet the creed of any great part of Christendom,' says one of the most distinguished commentators on 'Galatians' (Professor E. D. Burton); 'it never has been.'

But is it the creed whose hour has come—at the unlikeliest of times, in our generation, when we are seeing, as well as compassion and understanding of the human personality, a significant hardening of the ordering of society, a callousness and an imperviousness to more liberal influences; in fact, a sharpening of the issues? If this is God's time for it, are we under the same two temptations to evade it?

There are many in our churches, as we have suggested, for whom the 'Spirit' seems to be a comprehensive word for all the good that is in the hearts of men, the compassion and kindness, the concern for justice, the quest for truth. They would say, in varying ways, that there must be an origin for it; there must be a God from whom it has come. Jesus said so; and Jesus showed it in his life as no one else has ever done; and he also said that to take in the stranger, feed the hungry, clothe the naked, visit the sick and the prisoner, is to do it to him; and this is practical; this is faith.

But how many of these people believe, as the Bible must have us believe, in a power not our own, not contained within our human potentialities—a 'personal' Spirit who can be 'received', a power from beyond ourselves, giving a new dimension to life, and for the most part recognisably received because we are enabled to do what we have never done before, because we see something of the answering of prayer, because we find ourselves dramatically changed in our thinking?

How many must be uncomfortable when the reading of the Word of God sets all this out as basic to the Christian life? How many must take the tremendous words which the Scriptures apply to Jesus Christ as poetic descriptions, or forms of expression belonging to his generation and his Jewish background? What do they make of the New Testament declarations about the Cross and the Resurrection?

How many are there in our churches like that? They have a faith. They are standing, vaguely enough though it be, for something in the belief of the Church which the narrower, more fervent churchman can often be blind to. Ordinary men as they may be, they have a place in the Church. It is for them—and by implication it is for them in their ordinariness, for all that makes up their day-to-day ordinariness, the ordinary things of life. They are saying, by their presence if not by total belief, that the Holy Spirit is for the whole of life, for the life of the whole world—something which is not being said by a lot of believers. Their presence is a word of God to us. . . . And yet so much of the greatness, the mystery, the power of the Gospel has never come their way.

We sometimes rail at what brings these people into the

church at all—they show such little sign of understanding why they are there, what it is all about; they have to be perpetually urged to remember their duties, to undertake their responsibilities; they often look like a liability, giving a false impression to the outsider of what Christian belief is.

But some of us, by thinking and acting like that, increase the problems for them, even while we are faithfully keeping the church going. We have inherited a practice of faith. Our concern is to maintain it and encourage others to maintain it. We do not, on the whole, question what the 'great words' mean. We keep our Communion. We believe in some sense in the Spirit, without asking what more should be happening if the *power* of the Spirit were being received.

The presence of the apparently casual and formal member, against much influence which might keep him away, may be a sort of judgment against our rectitude—a rectitude which does not look for any new thing, anything more wonderful, anything more demanding, anything which would be a power to change us as well as other people. We may not appear to believe anything more than he does. He sees us holding on, without much thought, to the practices, the forms of thought, the language, the existing shape of the Church, with minds closed against any new thing God may be requiring of us. We are creating a settled Church when we need to be unsettled, a backward-looking Church when we need to be moving out where we have never gone before. This could be our form of bondage.

Paul raises fundamental questions for us. Is it the Spirit we discern, however vaguely, in our daily living in the world? And is it the same Spirit who gives us the 'salvation' which is in Christ, who opens the 'eyes of our understanding' to know Christ as a living Christ, to whom we can commit ourselves;

the same Spirit who is promised us in his power, although we ourselves may not be ready or willing to receive it? Are we confused like the Galatians between recognising the good which is in the world, which must be of God, and recognising the authentic Gospel faith and experience?

If it is the same Spirit, it must be one work. How are the different operations of the Spirit related to one another, so that we can see it as one work and stop dividing men who are responsive to his work in different areas and 'levels' of life into closed-off compartments—'good' Church members, 'nominal' Church members, 'outsiders'?

Why do we not receive the power of the Spirit as it is promised? Is it when, from two different kinds of misunderstanding, we fall into two categories: those who keep up the practices of the Faith but do not expect to receive 'power from on high', and those who see the Gospel only as a sort of ideal of what we should be trying to make of human life, a divine inspiration for the best of human effort? In both cases we are still in a kind of bondage; the one a bondage to the practices and traditions which we think we have to observe in order to be Christians; the other a bondage to the level of good which has been generally accepted (perhaps precariously) by the society around us. In both cases our effort is towards maintaining something which is less than a true Church of the Gospel of Christ.

Paul probes to the root of it with the question: 'How did you receive the Spirit?'

2 · Act of God

If the Gospel was Gospel it was the miracle of all miracles. It meant that God had written off the total evil in man—and proved it. The proof of it, says Paul, is in the power given to men to preach it—not quite the usual way of thinking of preaching today; but for Paul the true preaching of the Gospel had in it the same kind of miracle as the Cross and Resurrection. It was an immediate act of God. 'God called me through grace and chose to reveal his Son to me and *through* me.'

The *immediate* call and the *immediate* empowering to preach the Gospel belong to the same order as the finished work of Christ. Without the calling and the empowering, the miracle in Christ could not be known. There would be no 'power of God unto salvation'.

All is of God—the mercy, the remission of sins through the Cross, *and* the proclamation of it—*and* the believing. The preaching was not 'of human invention', not thought up by men's ingenuity of mind and skill of words, but a wisdom, an understanding, a power to open up the heart which was given as an immediate gift of God.

This was ultimately all that the preacher of the Gospel had

different from other men. Without that he was only one more thinker striving to out-think the doubters, a debater trying to show the reasonableness of the ideas that he was there to preach.

The Gospel was 'distorted' (Paul's word) when it was reduced to human argument, when men could weigh it up as any other opinion and give their own verdict; for what had happened was outside human experience and could not be understood in the light of human knowledge alone. The Cross and the Resurrection could not be known for what they were *from man's side*; they had to be seen from God's side; the Holy Spirit had to 'enlighten the eyes of the understanding' of men before they could see and believe. So the preaching, the enlightening, had to be of God, as the saving work of Christ had been of God, and the Resurrection the sign and seal of it.

It could not be philosophising, exhortation, moralising. It had to have in it the power to raise up belief, the power to break through what men were habituated into thinking, how they saw themselves and other men, how they assessed human life. It had to be a power to see what they had never seen before, to repent of what they had never thought to be wrong, to believe what they had never had it in them to believe. This was nothing less than a miracle of God's mercy. The power to believe was God's work in them; the preaching to enlighten their minds to Christ was God's work.

This word 'preaching' must have a wider meaning today. It is much more than one man's voice in a pulpit.

But this is the first stabbing question. Miracle in the preacher as well as miracle in the Gospel? Miracle in the preacher because of the use God makes of him, his words such as they are, not the 'eloquence of men's wisdom' but 'with power'; his own life a poor enough witness yet bearing about in him the evidence of what the dying of the Lord Jesus had meant. And from the miracle in the preacher to the miracle in the hearer, to be able to see what it is not given to men to see by the light of reason alone.

One proof of the Gospel, then, is in the power given to preach, and to hear and believe. The proof that this is of God, that the Holy Spirit is at work in us, is the same proof as the Church of the apostles had of his continuing work.

Evidence—that is what men need; and the first evidence must be that this happens, that the Holy Spirit is here with the same power as enabled Christ to 'humble himself and become obedient unto death, even the death of the Cross', the same power which raised him from the dead and 'gave him a name that is above every name'. If this power is not here, how can men at this distance in time believe in the power of the Cross and the Resurrection—and the forgiveness and new life and the promise of the Kingdom bound up in it?

That is Paul's question; and it comes when our minds, like the minds of the Galatian Christians, are being unsettled by many theories of human life and many theologies.

Why are we unsettled? Is it altogether a bad thing? Or is it part of the price we have to pay for going on to deeper truth—provided, as Paul would say, we do go on and do not get lost in what for him is another kind of Gospel?

It begins with the simple fact that the preacher has to understand the people to whom he is preaching, how they think, what influences them in the society in which they live, who are the objects of their admiration and anger, what their work does to them in creating a philosophy of how to deal with their fellow-men, what they think they are entitled to from 'life' (and therefore what they think life is for), what can be regarded as reasonable for men to be, and what is 'more than you can expect'.

The preacher comes by this knowledge partly by knowing himself and partly by being with other people. He must also read the signs of the times. He must know what interpretation is being put on events, what seems contrary to God's revealed will for men and what seems in accordance with it. He must know what the scientists are doing with the human personality, how they are manipulating mind and body for different measures of healing, how children are being taught to think, what kind of society men are capable of having, what policies are being advanced for it with widely different objectives. He reads the works of men who do not accept the Christian Gospel. He knows the influences of newspapers and television and radio. He must be realistic about the social changes which affect behaviour and character.

Most of this he would have to do in any case. He has to live in the same circumstances as everybody else. He has to converse, opinionate, assess, decide as they have to—although spared some of their severest work pressures. But he has also to be, in some humble degree, a prophet, an interpreter of what it all means; and for this he gathers in such wisdom as he can find in diverse quarters, an insight here, an experiment there, and here and there something which seems to throw light on what the Gospel should mean for living today—if indeed there is providence in this world of men, and judgment and love.

The 'unsettling' comes. What weight are we to give to these working philosophies by which men try to make their lives and their work manageable, tolerable and satisfying? And how does it all relate to the Gospel and all that it implies about what man is and is meant to be? Sin? Where is sin if not in these ordinary activities where we and other men are passing our judgments?

We try to find some settled point for our thinking in the signs of what God is doing in the world—this must have been the motivation of the Galatian Christians too. Why should there be love at all on our earth? Where has it come from? Why should there be search, however perverted and misdirected often, for some right way of life for mankind? Why should there be rebellion against injustice? Why should there be sacrifice? Why, in fact, should we bother about what happens to people—and be troubled about the homeless, and want to share our bread with the hungry?

These are signs, we say, of what we are meant to strive after. As Christians we declare it is because we are made in the image of God, however deformed the image may have become. So we make our claim and try to rally men to believe in it, and set it against the darker facts of cruelty and callousness and self-seeking.

We turn to the Gospels. The compassion of the Samaritan in the parable is not only good but God-like. The impulse to feed the hungry, visit the sick, welcome the stranger, go to the man in prison is more than an urge in men; it is God urging men.

This is our claim: that this is God's world—that there is a providence, a purpose, a judgment and Fatherly love at the heart of all. And yet we are still unsettled, like the Galatians.

We can reach a point, on the one hand, where we take all the evidence of compassion and caring for men, their struggle for freedom and justice, their anger against hurt done to little children, their passion to search for truth—and call it 'God'. We can take Jesus as the supreme example of it—the Master, the Lord, 'in some sense' Son of God, done to death because men were not ready for love at that height and depth. We can adapt the great words of Scripture to be the supreme description of what we can as yet see only faintly in the life of ordinary men: the Cross—forgiving love at its ultimate; the Resurrection—death not the end; 'reconciliation'—men learning to live together in the spirit of Christ and in harmony with God's will; the 'liberty of the children of God'—a release from the evils which deprive and pervert and destroy; the 'new life in Christ'—the loving of our neighbour as ourselves.

And then men say fairly enough: 'What is there here we didn't know?' Preaching has become no more than encouragement in what they already know, exhortation to live up to it.

What has got lost (Paul's word)? What is it that the preacher is not doing?

What has gone out is the power of the Spirit—the power of God; the Gospel that it was the power of God which came with Jesus in human weakness; that it was the power of God which worked miracles through him; that the Cross was the power by which sinful men were restored to the Father; that it was by the power of God that Jesus was raised from the dead; that it was the power of God which came upon men at Pentecost—the power to believe, the power to repent of what seemed inevitable, basic to human nature; the power to live the 'new life in Christ' in the worst circumstances of this world's life; the power to save the world 'through him'.

If the Gospel is not being preached in this power men are in fact being called to do what the Scriptures say they cannot do. It is a denial of what the Scriptures say—that it is only by the power of the Spirit that we can believe and obey the Gospel.

'How have you received the Spirit?' By assessing the signs in human life that there must be a God of love? By the evidence that men are made to be good, that life is made for love and for caring, that mankind is made to be one family? Or have you received the Spirit by the immediate act of God, by the 'enlightening of the eyes of your understanding' to know him here in mercy and judgment? We can see *signs* of the Spirit, and be responsive to some of them and resistant to others—but can we receive the *power* of the Spirit by any other way than the immediate act of God?

Yet we can also, in trying to recover the Gospel from man-made wisdom, put ourselves under the other temptation, the temptation of the Judaizers in Galatia. We can turn to urging men back into conformity, to do the right things, to have the right practice of belief, to have the right words for it, to accept what was good enough for our fathers, to be dutiful in the work and worship of the Church—in fact, to do what seems to keep us right with God but in fact closes our minds against the miracle of his grace, this immediate power to live a life impossible to ordinary, sinful human nature.

Because of this built-in capacity for getting the right things wrong we need to be always going back to our Lord himself.

3 · How did Jesus see it?

Jesus was baptised 'of the Spirit' when (can we say 'because'?) he stood with that motley crowd of sinful men and women on the banks of Jordan, making himself one with them. He was 'baptised' into the sacrifice of the Cross for the bearing of the sins of the world. ('I have a baptism to be baptised with and how am I straitened until it be accomplished'.)

The baptism of the Cross was in one sense a solitariness, in another the complete identification with men in the life of the world. 'One died for all', because the whole life of men was in him; and it was the whole life of men that was redeemed.

A great mystery—and yet he himself speaks of the Spirit with simplicity and explains how his disciples are to be 'in' the world but not 'of' the world.

How did he see the world God had created? The providence? The signs were there in the life of men.

The Father, for Jesus, is clearly to be seen in the life provided for men ('If God so clothe the grass of the field . . . will he not clothe you, O ye of little faith?'). God is in the impulse of the shepherd to go searching for the lost sheep. God is in the zest of the merchant, setting his heart on the best pearl.

The compassion and the caring is in men because God has made them so.

When we argue from the love which is in men to the love which must have created them we have Jesus with us. ('If ye then, being evil, know how to give good gifts unto your children will not your heavenly Father give good gifts to them that ask him?'). God is in the home, in that impulse. God is in the play of the children. God is at the family table.

It is because God has created men in his own image that men are to learn how to live together and share what he provides. It is because men are made for God that they have to find that the nation which orders their daily affairs must fulfil his purposes or be destroyed. It is because God is here that we believe human life is meant to be lived in one kind of way rather than another—in serving rather in than overlording, in sacrifice rather than in self-seeking, in the reconciling of differences rather than in division. Even without a full Christian faith we can discern that.

So we get this answer first of all, justifying us in reasoning from this kind of presence in the world to the kind of God he must be.

But why is this not enough—to live up to this belief to the best of our power? The second answer we get seems sharply different. Jesus says 'Repent'. It is not a question of 'to the best of our power', because there is an enemy in our midst; there is an enemy within us, fighting against what God has put into creation, turning us away from what he means us to be if we are to inherit the kingdom prepared for us. Our powers are not sufficient for that fight. These other forces within us are too strong. We often do not see the evil because it is confusedly mixed up with the good. The impulses which are from God become corrupted; love turns to jealousy; the zeal for the right is twisted into pride that we are doing the right; the zest of doing the work of God's world becomes self-advancement at the expense of others.

In spite of all the signs of good and of God, the second answer we get from Jesus is that word 'Repent'; and the repentance is not only for the more intimate of our personal relationships where we love and 'get it wrong' and need to forgive and be forgiven; it is just as much for the world of work, the conversation of work, the motives and the methods of work, what we make of our living together in our communities, what kind of nation and world we build up by our work.

Jesus says we are out of our depth. The evil is in us, part of us; we are sinful men and women; and the 'best of our power' will not lift us out of the condition we are in. 'Repent' means 'You can't do it'.

It is the very complexity of it that tempts us to give up and resign ourselves just to being as decent as we can; all that can be expected of us in such a world as this, fallen from what it was intended to be. We have to adapt ourselves, make the best we can of it, and keep before us as an ideal for the future what God meant to be a present reality. 'He will understand . . . he will be compassionate . . . he knows what we are up against.'

The third word of Jesus pierces right through that. It is the simple word 'Ask'. What are we to ask for is the Holy Spirit—which means that God can do this very thing we say is impossible for us. The Holy Spirit of the baptism of Jesus is for us, and it is for the whole of life, for the places where we think the life which God has ordained for us cannot reasonably be expected of us, where we say we have to compromise, adapt ourselves to the standards of the people around us, the way men's work has been organised, the way the community and nation have been ordered. This is to be the beginning of the Kingdom—on earth as in heaven. The meaning of the Kingdom is that it is the life of God shared with his children now. So to say 'impossible' is to say that the Kingdom is impossible on earth; it is to say, not that *we* cannot do it but that God cannot.

In face of the complexity and intricacy of human evil and human despair we are to do something so simple that it is *too* simple. We are to speak to God precisely when we think nothing can come of it, because we cannot see how he can do for us what we need. We are to speak just when we are thinking that, if there is a God of love, he must be a God in the background, or at least a God with a love which cares but cannot do for us what he would wish to do—only a watching, compassionate, sorrowful God. But Jesus said that the Father whom we are to ask is a Father who can do the impossible—enable us to begin to learn the life of the Kingdom here, in the worst circumstances, in the situations which deny it. We are to love our enemies while they are still enemies—because that is what God is doing. We are to learn what is for the common good along with men who seem to be 'out for themselves'. We are to speak the word of self-control and patience in retort to the word of anger. We are to pray for those who treat us unjustly and 'deserve all they get'. We are to forgive them when forgiving seems weakness, to be humble in the presence of the overbearing, to be 'meek' when the power and the authority is being given to the self-confident, to be peacemakers when the obvious and reasonable thing is to keep the barriers up or at best to agree to differ.

We are to ask and to trust—that is being like a child. A child does not think out all the reasons why he should trust his father, and from the sum of it all decide to trust. His trust is an action before it is an argument—his father is to be trusted. He does not think out how much there must be for him to learn from his father; he turns to his father and trusts he will get what he needs.

This is too simple for us in our sophistication. So it becomes difficult. We make it difficult.

One attempted escape from the difficulty is to think that the Holy Spirit is given only for our relationship with God—setting us right with him. But it is the world that has gone wrong; and what is wrong in us belongs to the world which has gone wrong. Our sin and the sin of the world are one. Our turning from God is the same turning which happens in the world's work.

This is not for our 'inner life' only; it is for the whole of our life, the whole of our conversation, the whole of our conduct, the whole of our effort. The reason why we will not be more simple is that our sin has made us more and more complicated; and the life of the world makes us more complicated every day; and the simple thing is the thing we are less and less able and ready to do.

It is not enough, therefore, to read the signs of God in the world and be thankful for them; and to attempt to base our faith on them alone. We have also to recognise the signs of the denial of God—how deeply they go in ourselves and in the life around us, the enemy within and the enemy without—and the power of that enemy as Jesus saw it; working against God and turning good to evil. We have to take our Lord's word for it. He knew it as we cannot know it.

When he says 'Turn to God' it means more than 'Learn to look at your life in a different way—educate yourself to a different way of living'; it means 'Turn, for your life'—save your life. He speaks of the snake escaping from a racing fire. He speaks of destruction. He speaks of life and death.

When he says 'Ask' it means more than 'Put this in as one of your petitions in prayer'; it means 'Ask for this in desperation'. He speaks about men hammering on their neighbour's door; men clamouring to be heard; men who know they must be heard. And the proof of the urgency is in himself.

Gethsemane is to come; Calvary is to come. In Gethsemane the tortuous sins of the world are borne in on him, and thrust into the Father's heart. This is what the Son is to bear in the Father's name. The death on the Cross—the baptism into sacrifice for the sins of men—is the sum of all the elaborate perversion into which men have turned God's gift of life. It is complex beyond all understanding. But the act of our saving has in it a terrible simplicity: the offering of the innocent for the guilty, the one for the many. Asking with his life, his all, for our sakes, he makes simple in sacrifice what men have made intricate in sin.

It is a terrifying simplicity—this mercy of God—until our eyes are opened to understand what it means. It is the kind of simplicity which our minds must consider impossible—until we believe. And yet Jesus turns from speaking about the Cross ('This he said, signifying by what death he should glorify God') to saying to us 'your cross'—'Whosoever is not willing to take up his cross daily is not worthy to be my disciple'. Something of that great and terrible simplicity is to be in us.

The explanation of how it is to happen is Pentecost. There the fullness of God is laid open to sinful men—just to receive, to accept without assessing how it can possibly be, knowing only that it is because Christ has died for our sins, and is risen; taking what we have no right to take, taking like a child, trusting like a child, asking like a child, taking holiness into our sinfulness, taking the simplicity of the 'amazing love of God'. How could the Father dwell in men even as he had dwelt in Christ? This was the question to which Pentecost gives the answer. This is the consummation. It is the very Spirit of the crucified and glorified Jesus given to men, the power of the Spirit, the power which raised Christ from the dead, baptism in that power.

It is for the whole of life—for new peace with God, a new way opened up between God and men, but also new life for the world, for the whole of creation, for the work by which men live, for their living together in community—and for their hope of the heavenly kingdom.

For the apostolic church it was immediately about how men earned and spent their money; what they did with their possessions and how much of possessions they should have; how they dealt with employer and employee; how far they were to obey, and where they were to disobey, law and order; what they were to do with aliens. It was power to live the new life in these situations—guidance about where they were to go, what they were to say, how they were to relate their own living to the living of other men who were not believers, how they were to share with their poorer brethren, how they were to suffer in silence in some situations and in others to speak with boldness against the authority entrenched in the State—in fact, how to live a life of trust in a suspicious world, a life of forgiveness in a world of retaliation, a life of faith in God in a world where human nature has elaborated the rules and tightened its systems to conform to its own type of predestination. This was turning the worst in human relationships to the best, to the glory of God.

The outpouring of the Spirit is the consummation of the act

of God by which the world is saved in its total life—not individual men only but men in their communities and nations, men making decisions, men in their trading, men in their use and misuse of the powers of nature, men making decisions about the use of their own powers.

It is, by human standards, an impossible simplicity, this receiving of the Spirit, for men whose minds are, as they think, secure only in their own ways, within the complexity of the world's life, manipulating its expertise for their complicated ends. It is 'terrible' because it means a different thinking, being impelled to look at the whole human elaboration from the single point of what has been shown us in Christ.

4 · How does it happen?

In many different ways; but always there is something in common.

I believed, as I thought, in the Gospel, the love of God revealed in Christ, the promise of eternal life. The Gospel was a kind of over-all guide; but it did not give help in the particular moment when I had to put my word into somebody else's mind and take his word into mine, and make my decision —in fact in the shaping of the day's work.

My Damascus road—and it was on a road—was when I was making an act of forgiveness, as I thought, towards a fellow-worker in Christ's Church; standing beside him, as I considered, in brotherly love; being merciful, in spite of what he had done to me.

I needed the forgiveness of God too; but deep down in me I felt that some other people needed it more; and he was one of them. I was measuring up my standing with God alongside his. I was still counting on merit—especially the merit of being able to forgive. I saw myself suddenly in that condition. I was judging while I was forgiving. I was standing on the other side, because I had achieved a standing with God. But in that moment when my eyes were opened I knew I was standing absolutely alongside this man I had been judging. There was no measuring of his need against mine. We were together in the same need, whatever the arguments might be about what he had said and I had said and the measure of right and wrong which had been in them. As human beings, as Christians, we stood together, nothing separating us, up or down, in our need of what Christ had done for us.

How had I come to see that? By thinking it out? By conscience? I knew it was not. God had opened my eyes.

I cannot believe that such insights are entirely my own—my self-knowledge. They come at the very moment when another motive is dominant, just when I am sure of myself, when I am certain I am right. They are an uncovering of what I do not believe to be there in me. It is against my will that I see myself like this. Yet, once seen, it has a quite contradictory thankfulness in it, a sense of God, an assurance that this is one more evidence of what is being worked out of my system by a power not my own which has the marks of the love of Christ in it—God in Christ.

My eyes had been opened. God was here now. This was his doing—and it was for both of us together. I am telling how it happened, not to say 'This is how it must always happen', but to try to show the essential in it. It was the sudden sight of someone as God saw him. It was not this man who had touched my heart. It was God.

What is the 'something in common' which we experience in the Holy Spirit in those decisive moments? It is this para-doxical blend of being 'shown up' and shown the new man we are to be—shame and hope, the revelation of the depth and intricacy of the evil in us, but along with it the absolute certainty that he who has shown us the depths is he who is here to raise us up to new heights. The judgment and the mercy and the grace are one in him—and they become one in us. We see a new brother. We get the power to speak new words to him. We do new things. We have new relationships. We have the love of Christ as new impulse and objective.

All is of God. That is Paul's claim; and it does not mean that the Spirit has not been at work in us until those moments. It is because of the Spirit that I am moved by compassion, even if I am still secretly commending myself for being compassionate. It is because of the Spirit that I am uncomfortable when I have 'fallen out' with someone and want to 'make it up', even if there is also the motive of removing an embarrassment. It is because of the Spirit that I do not press home too sorely a wrong someone has done, even if in excusing the other man I am also excusing myself and my own faults. I have had the Spirit; the Spirit is within us; it is not that something more of the Spirit is given; it is that something more of me is given to the Spirit and I receive power for the work of Christ—more power from the Spirit who has been with me in fullness.

Being 'filled' with the Spirit, the New Testament tells us, is receiving of the fullness of God—but I had not believed in what the fullness could mean. Now I had asked for the whole truth; been willing to take it—and the miracle of the power had happened, a particular baptism of the Spirit for this particular moment, this particular work of Christ. I had begun to want to know what that work was for myself as well as for him. I was beginning to want to know how Christ saw us both.

I learned from this not to worry so much about my mixed motives but to ask quite simply to be taken in hand, to be ready to believe that, as John says, I can become 'like him' in this very situation I am in, ready to be changed into that likeness, whatever it cost, to believe that this is there for me.

I know that when I make a gesture of admitting a fault I am probably secretly proud of meeting the man half-way with whom I have been differing. I know that my peacemaking is often the kind that pays, and saves my position and makes my work easier. I know that I find it convenient sometimes to let a wrong-doer off lightly and earn his gratitude and liking. I know that when I make a stand for justice and right I am gaining a public reputation for forthrightness and boldness of speech. My good and my bad are all mixed up. But anxiety about it will do me no good; and the effort to cleanse my motives simply does not work. Worse still, I am confused between what help God can give and what must come from myself in trying to do better.

This is the point where I either go on in my confusion, my resignation to all kind of mixed motives (more and more covered up), my acceptance of my human nature (and aren't we all more or less like this?)—or 'ask, believing'?

And what am I asking for? This is the crux. Is it 'help' only, help to get me out of these difficulties one by one? Or is it the 'fullness of God', the Holy Spirit, the whole truth for the moment I am in? Of course it is true that I am asking for what I already have. The Spirit has been given. But by my asking I am making myself readier for his power.

The fullness of God means the total love of God—all that was in Christ, the power that was given to Christ because he bore our sins and because he understands us to the depths. And to ask, even without knowing all that I am asking for, is to be that much more willing to be empowered.

I must not worry about how sincere, how fervent, how

urgent, how persuasive, my asking is—that is to turn it over once again into something which depends on me—the strength of my desire, the honesty of my repentance, my determination to live a new life, the rightness of the way I think of my belief, the power of my prayer. All this has to be of God, not of ourselves. What is for us is the simple thing which a child does—to ask, without analysing what kind of asking it is; to take without needing to know first everything about what we are receiving; to be ready for what is given because we need it; to act impulsively when we know we are seeing the Christ-like thing, having faith that it is Christ-like.

This is the crux, because we are asking, whether we think into all that it means at first or not, for the love of Christ. We are not asking to be able to believe the *idea* of the love of Christ, to be helped to accept it as a reasonable hypothesis for living. We are asking for the love itself—because the asking makes us ready to receive it. This is how we receive the Spirit's power; and if it means love it means wanting our brother to receive it along with us.

We do not need to know all that it means; it 'passes knowledge', the New Testament says. All that we need is to want what we see in Christ—in his death for us, in his resurrection for us. The fullness will unfold—the discovery how real his love is to the very things we have to say and do, and therefore how real God is in every part of our lives, how close to us is what Christ lived and died and was raised from the dead to do. It is a love which is realistic to the point of hurt—love which can hurt piercingly by opening our eyes to see ourselves and other people as we are, love which can be 'angry' (to use our inadequate human word), love which can give urgent understood rebuke when we are willing to recognise it, love which can give compelling, recognisable directive, love which can encourage, with incredible understanding of the innermost nature of our frailty and failure, love which is always seeing us as we are to be in the kingdom of his glory through the travail of his soul and yet also as we are now—actually receiving this love, taking it into our lives, being taken up into it . . . otherwise it is not love, and the Scriptures are misleading us when they speak of a loving God.

By that day's happening I was brought back to those words 'power' and 'preaching'. (We shall see later the necessary extension of 'preaching' in our day beyond the 'one man: one pulpit'). My own preaching—what kind of power was it intended to have?

I had learned three things about God in this one moment of time. First, that he had been at work in me before I knew I was being called to this depth of ministry. Second, that he had gone on with this work in patience and mercy while I had been resisting much of what he was requiring of me. Third, that it was he who had brought me to this hour.

Those to whom the apostles were first sent saw enough in the life, death and resurrection of Christ and in the signs of the fellowship of his Church to make them want to say 'God'. Then they were ready to be shown the something more which enabled them to see Christ as the one sent to save them from their sins, to stand for them before the Father so that they could be accepted in him. The way was prepared. The Holy Spirit had opened their eyes—they could not have seen this for themselves; and to know that their eyes had been opened was to open their whole life to the Spirit, to be ready to receive him. He had brought them to that hour.

I knew, like that, that my eyes had been opened; that it was the Holy Spirit who had shown me what I could never have seen for myself—and, in knowing that, I was ready for anything more he had to show me and for the power to do it; I was ready to receive him as I had never been before—the fullness of God was opening up before me.

And there was this also, so unbelievable until now: this other man and myself were inseparably involved in what the Holy Spirit had done. My acceptance of him was one with my being accepted in Christ. It was for both of us. We had to learn from one another, through one another, in the very situation which had driven us apart. This was how the Holy Spirit worked in us, when we were ready for this too, ready for our brother as well as for God.

This was why there must be 'foolishness' in my preaching— 'foolishness' for anyone looking for nothing more than a reasonable, common-sense view of life.

But what could have seemed foolish about my preaching? That God loves us? That God forgives? That God has a fatherly care over us? That God helps us?

That could not sound astonishing, unbelievable, a shock to our intelligence. It was an interpretation of human life I could expect people to accept and be helped by—at the level of human wisdom.

The power which was at work between that man and me was the power of God taking the wrong in both of us into himself and not only clearing it away as if it had not existed but actually creating new men out of it.

I had preached that Christ prayed on the Cross 'Father, forgive them'—but it was the *answer* to that prayer which held the power. I had preached that he had offered himself in sacrifice for the sins of the world—but it was the *answer* to the sacrifice, what 'happened' in the heart of God, that held the power: the Resurrection, the 'power of the Resurrection'. Pentecost was the answer. The preaching of the Gospel, in the power of the Spirit, with power to change the lives of men, was the answer.

The cry after Pentecost was not 'Jesus has shown us what kind of men we are to be' but 'Christ has set us free'.

This was the foolishness, and still is. This is what is unbelievable to ordinary reason, and still is—that by the act of one man we are in a relationship to God where our sin does not cut us off from him as it ought to. It is not that what we are does not separate us from God. It does. We have in us what he hates. We think and do what is a violation of the kingdom of heaven. We go against the very nature of his being in the motives we harbour and encourage in ourselves. It is not that all this is overlooked. We *are* actually separated by what is in us. His mercy is not that he excuses us. His mercy is that he has taken what he does hate, what does separate us from him, and made it his own—so that he can look at it at its very worst through his eyes and deal victoriously with it. This was what the Son of God brought into the Father's heart. And the power which broke out, the mercy, the Spirit poured out on men, is the miracle which is the Gospel—but a terrible miracle, a 'great and terrible love', because this forgiveness means that the worst that is in us has been taken into the heart of God, as the Cross is in the heart of God. The separation is there—and not allowed to separate. The sin is there, overcome by undeserved grace.

This is the miracle to be received in trembling because of what it means. This is what the 'fear of the Lord' is—so much misunderstood; no mere staving off of punishment; but going deeply into the receiving of the love of God. Our trembling becomes, strangely, power.

This is where the power comes from—and from nowhere else. All is of God because all is *in* God. This is why we can receive the Spirit—because the power from the heart of God is in the world. And nothing less than this is the power given us to repent and believe through the preaching of the Gospel. Only this can create true contrition and faith in us.

This is the power which broke out from the Cross, the power which is given us to live a new life, because we are released into it along with Christ. It is his kind of power, not the world's.

My preaching had not been in that power. I had not had expectancy in it. My own asking had not had expectancy in it as I prepared to preach. I do not know what kind of power I had thought of as belonging to true preaching—but it had not been this kind of power, the power of the Spirit seizing men in all sorts of conditions like mine and that man's, and changing their whole outlook, not merely making us think again and differently but think and speak and act as we had never done to each other before—because we were freed to do it. Sinful men as we still were, we were treated as if we were fit for the highest. Even as we were, we were getting the inmost thoughts of God. We were being taken into the impulses of perfect love, into the 'holy of holies', as if we had a right to belong there. We were being given the intimate words for our need, as if they were 'natural' to God's own way of thinking and not the result of an incredible descent into the depravity of our motives and reactions.

This was what the apostles had to shout about—this astonishing thing: men taken to be now what they were not; men called free while they were still very plainly not free in the sense in which they used the word.

Men had been given a standing with God to which they had no right; men were being called sons of God because the Son of God had made them brothers; men were coming under the mercy of God before they had repented and become able to believe in the mercy.

This was the power of the Gospel; and the power that was to be in men believing and preaching in the power of the Spirit; not to be taken as 'encouragement' of an ordinary kind, or comfort of an ordinary kind, but something to be taken as unbelievable and yet able to be proved true.

This was the 'glorious liberty of the children of God'— which is first of all freedom from guilt, freedom from a relationship with God which the Scriptures call enmity; and, only because of that, freedom from the tension and the fear, the insecurity and false facades of wrong relationship with other people.

Christ has freed us from the impossibility of 'working our passage' into right relationship with God (for the Judaizers, by the observance of the Law). And, if we know and believe this, we are free to begin to learn also what it is to be free between one another, and what a society of free men ought to be like.

This is why Paul's question to the Galatians is for me. How have I come to believe? By the word of men, the wisdom of men, the cogency of an argument that there must be a God of love—or by this power given me by God himself, which is the same power as was in Christ, here now for me in the Spirit?

5 · Where does it happen?

It can happen when we are alone—and unprepared for it; as with Paul, God 'apprehending us'. It can happen when we are with believing people, in church, in a group where the Spirit is so obviously at work that we are caught up into his undeniable presence and power. It can happen because we are being prayed for; and the central mystery of the Kingdom is come upon us. All this is in the records.

But the Spirit is given for our life in the world. We do not 'receive' the Spirit in some special place and work out by ourselves what it ought to mean in the practicalities of our work and our home. That would be back to ourselves again at the very points where we are under the severest pressure to conform to the life around us. The Spirit is for the battle against the world's evil—where it hits us.

Of course there are many levels of human activity, beginning with the simplest physical routines. We are not engaged equally as persons at all levels. There is work which is the carrying out of straightforward duties without reference to other people. There is conversation on work which is concerned only with the exchange of facts. There is meeting with people which requires no more than courtesy and politeness. There is casual conversation in the light-hearted hour, although in all this we are no doubt unconsciously revealing what we are. But there are also points where much more is at stake. There is the moment when we are determined to push aside our scruples, to concentrate on the mechanics of an argument. Is this just ambition for the firm or company—success, development? Or has it suddenly become a judgment on the values of human life, the human as he is meant to be, the human as God means him to be treated, the neighbour at the other side of the world, the brother 'for whom Christ died'? Is this why the determination to take our own way in that moment has to grow harder in order to achieve its purpose—because we are going against God—God present with us? The sin not just against the moral principle but against him ('Against thee, thee only, have I sinned').

I have had times when I was made aware of precisely this kind of hardening.

There was another breakdown in relationship, different from the one I have already referred to (my own share of responsibility being different). The man with whom I was working was bent on achieving certain objectives, regardless of opposition. He was prepared to over-rule and over-ride any questioning of his policy. He counted on displays of anger making me compliant 'for peace sake'. I had some understanding of what had caused him to be like this; but when it came to false statements being made and other people being involved in strain and tension I hardened. He could not be allowed to 'get away with it'.

But suddenly one day I saw that I was hardening myself, not against this man and what he was doing but against God and what he wanted me to be to this man, the words I was to say, the honesty between myself and himself which was needed so that rights and wrongs could be talked about without becoming totally 'him' and 'me'. It was against this that I was hardening myself—against what God wanted and was showing me; and the more he wanted it the harder I had to be in my resistance to him. And I saw that this must often be happening. I had to put into my relationship with this man the kind of love Jesus had towards men, the kind of love that led to his death.

But how am I to be ready for these moments, watchful for the warning or the impulse? This is where self has to be 'denied', if I am to follow Christ; and it has to be denied at the very moment when it does not seem possible for it to be denied, when arguments are unanswerable, when I am standing for my rights, when it surely seems permissible to deal with this other man on the ground he has chosen. But if the Spirit is there with us in these issues of the world's working life this one thing is certain. If I am under temptation at the points where I feel I have everything on my side, where I move over imperceptibly into the world's way of thinking, it is away *from him*. It is *against him*.

Then there must be the possibility of being saved there. If I can be deflected off course from him it must be that he can bring me back on course. The Spirit of God is there to be lost but there to be found: where I brace my will against his, where I try to close my mind against him, where I thrust aside the thoughts which have come from him, where I become more and more determined to have my way. I am acknowledging him in the determination I must summon up for the denial.

On the other side, when I have the impulse to forgive, to help the man who does not want to be helped, to say what I know must be said even if it will be resisted, to do what is right because I see that it is right in God's sight although it goes against the grain in me to do it, the power of the Spirit is being given—not just because I have remembered a word from Scripture, but because the Spirit is there to remind me of the word and to make it a living impulse, because he is there with a mind for the very thing I am doing or not doing, a mind thinking along with mine, able to correct, guide and rebuke in a way I can understand. This is why I become able to find in people what I never expected, what they did not mean to reveal and yet were meant to reveal, suddenly giving depth to a conversation. This is the Spirit coming in power.

It would be strange if new life in Christ did not sometimes have evidence of a newness so dramatically different that we have to cry 'My Lord and my God'; but it can be there almost unobserved.

This is the only explanation I have for what happens when I ring a door-bell and ask for the wisdom or the comfort which I know I do not have it in me to give; or as I lift the telephone to speak to a man in despair when no words of mine can relieve; or as I take up my pen to write to a woman so embittered that no pleading, no argument, can reach—he is there to use my useless words and make them the means of accomplishing what he alone can do. The useless words are needed. They become more than my compassion.

This is power beyond our power and beyond ordinary experience. It takes in what we do not know. It prepares us for what could not otherwise be in us. It moves the hearts— and the feet—of people we have never met. It alters motives in people without a word of any kind from us. It brings a man where he had made up his mind not to go, where he hears a Gospel he had been determined to resist. It raises up the impulse of forgiveness where something had been done which could never be forgiven. It moves people along streets to houses which they did not mean to enter ever again. It gives a sentence in the Bible the power to make a man believe. It enables us to believe that what is there in Scripture can happen now, because the Spirit of God is here to accomplish it. Without that the Gospel becomes an episode in history, however important; and faith means taking Jesus only as an example and an ideal, and belief mainly intellectual acceptance of the Church.

The Spirit is the miracle of the Gospel brought to me hour by hour, sometimes recognisable and demanding my obedience in his love, sometimes at work unrecognised—especially if it is reaching me through other people. This is the triumph of the Cross; and the awakening of my love for him. And I become open to receive the Spirit where I am standing by other men, where I am with my brother, as I was on that road when the power of the Spirit came on me—where I am at work, where I am involved with other people in the crucial issues of life. The Spirit is given for life in the world as it is.

Is this too simple for us, for the realities of business, the plans to be fixed, the people to be held in conversation, the decisions to be taken?

It does not mean that problems are solved for us without effort and struggle and perseverance. We may have to see a situation more intricately rather than less. We may discover that the additional involvement with people at a new depth at first means greater complications.

The simplicity is not in a deliverance from the complications of our human society; it is in being open to learn, open to correction, open to direction from the Spirit who knows the hearts of all men. It is the simplicity of love, in which we learn the difficult things together. The Gospel is simple; but the new life in Christ, however 'easy' the yoke, has to be lived where men have made life far more tortuous than God meant it to be; and we have to work through the complexities with them.

The simplicity and the complexity are to be seen every time we sit round the supper table as a family. We come home in the evening with the impress of different work on us, reacting to our experiences, perhaps divided sharply in what we think right and reasonable for teenagers to do, for parents to do, for the family to do as a family. Our talk represents a complex world. When we get into argument it will almost certainly be over individual interpretations of how our sector of the world is being run, over politics, over rights and wrongs in somebody's relationship with somebody else, something said, something done, open to judgment; all entangled in our opinions, in assertion of ourselves, in the interaction of our personalities. And yet there is something in common. We are bound together by the word we seldom mention on our lips but use as a sort of 'coda' to our letters to one another. Our love has its strains and its misunderstandings; its withdrawals, its enigmatic silences; but it is basically simple, however mysterious.

The complexity of the world, the 'practicalities', the ambitions, the decisions—they are all there; and yet at the heart of the family circle this apparently precarious but dependable strength, as we bring ourselves together and give ourselves one to another and to the possibility of love—at God's depth.

Here we are, around the table—what we are because God has made us like this, capable of the sensitiveness from which can come both love and anger; giving ourselves, withdrawing ourselves. Here we are, with what we have made of ourselves in living and working with others; what we would wish to do and cannot do, wish to be and cannot be. And here is that other dimension, if the Gospel is true: what can be made of us by the work of the Holy Spirit on us; our impossible which is God's possible; the complexity of our lives, which makes sin to so easily 'beset us', brought to this point of simplicity.

The very deviousness of our conversation and defensiveness ('I gave him as good as I got . . . If I don't look after my interests who will? . . . That's something I'll never forgive')—this is part of the evidence that what is evil and against God is woven into our thinking and conversation. We cannot get ourselves out of it just by trying to knock off this or that bad habit. We have to be cleansed; we have to be new, with the simplicity of the love of Christ. This is what we have to prepare for.

And there is also another sign of the new dimension (again, two people); 'What things soever ye desire, when ye pray, believe that ye receive them, and ye shall have them'. That is the simplicity of the Gospel transferred over to us. It is not by going over the problems and the arguments and assessing them that we receive, but first of all by simple asking—the asking for God himself, for help for what we may not think we need help for, asking for all that is ours because we are Christ's and Christ is God's; asking which centres on the promise of the Holy Spirit. ('. . . how much more will your heavenly Father . . .')

The Cross of Christ was judgment on all the outworking and inworking of human sin in such detail and solidarity that it could not be seen for what it was, and there was just no way to deal with it, even if there had been the will. The simplicity was in his giving of himself for us.

I must expect to be as he was in the world, where human sin gets more and more involved in the work by which men live, in the development of their powers, in the more and more complicated processes of their knowledge. I must do more than know that this is also in me. I must ask. It must be simple repentance, whatever complexity there may be in my sinful actions. It must be simple belief, because I am believing in a Christ who humbled himself for me to that simplicity of becoming 'obedient unto death . . . even the death of the Cross'.

There must be in me some simple cry of the heart to meet that simple cry in him. Every day will have its complexities. But it is in that simplicity that I must make all my beginnings. 'He loved me and gave himself for me'. There is nothing simpler than that.

We distort the Gospel if we are so caught up in the philosophies of men, in their sciences, in their theories (perhaps with the best of intentions to understand the world we are living in and to be 'able to give an answer to them that ask . . .') until the simple fact of being accepted by God 'in Christ' (as the Scriptures say) ceases to be a miracle of mercy and grace, from which new life for men springs, and the whole world becomes a new creation.

If men are wrong, creation is wrong, because it is one creation, one inter-relationship, one belonging together. If men are put right, creation is put right. The fact of men being put right with God in the Cross and Resurrection of Christ is fact for the whole scientific world we live and work in as well as for the souls of men.

6 · The proof is outside

'How do you receive the Spirit?' was Paul's question. 'By the preaching of the Gospel' was the short answer.

But this for him was a good deal more than our fifteen minutes at '11' and '6.30'. Behind that word 'preaching' was the testimony of the apostles and a people praying that the power of prophetic utterance would be given to the preacher, the power to believe given to the hearers. There were the indisputable facts of what was happening 'in the power of the Spirit'. There was the steady incoming of a very mixed company of men and women, being accepted as brothers and sisters in spite of their status in society, and their nationality and race.

'How do you receive the Spirit?' The answers in the book of 'Acts' are in words strange to our generation. But we cannot eliminate from our Bibles what happened without destroying Scripture. 'Repent and believe'; 'Believe on the Lord Jesus Christ and thou shalt be saved'; 'Believe in God that raised Jesus up from the dead'.

The word 'believe' for many has come to seem like an intellectual assent to a theory about who Jesus was and what he signified. It may look unreasonable or almost irrational that quite suddenly in 'Acts' a man should be asked to say what he 'believed', on the briefest of testimonies of one of the apostles.

But 'Believe' meant 'Come and see for yourself'—a simple, practical proof—as well as the miracle of the Spirit creating sudden conviction between two minds. They were to come along the road to a house and find themselves being accepted at a level they had never known before, into a fellowship where all things were held in common. 'Nothing short of a miracle', they must have said. That was it—part of the miracle, the visible evidence, the proof of what would otherwise have been a mystical experience for the few who were 'made that way'. They found the mystery that they were accepted of God in Christ by the sheer miracle that they were accepted like that by these Christians.

So the question 'How do you receive the Spirit?' has two answers. The first is that it is by the immediate act of God— the miracle of grace, the power of his presence 'in fullness'. This is what the Book of 'Acts' declares; and, if we doubt that there was that kind of presence and power then, we will not believe that it is here now.

The second answer is that for many it was 'Come and see'— come and be convinced. If we cannot say that, it is either because we have not got it to say, or are not going out to say it—and the apostles would declare that if the second is not happening the first cannot be.

Is it that we have been intellectualising the Gospel? Have we been making 'Repent and believe' seem like intellectual assent to one possible interpretation of human life—on the evidence of Scriptures written a long time ago?

We preach the incarnation of Jesus, taking upon himself to

be in all things as we are. But do we believe and act on the belief that the Holy Spirit takes upon himself, takes into himself, every human motive, every feeling, every impulse, every reaction, every anger, every love as it is in us, and is with us to transform, to turn and change our minds, to show us what to seek, what to believe, how to accept our brother, what to say to him, what to do for him? This is the incarnating of the Holy Spirit.

If we have not been 'out there', accepting men as very part of our accepting Christ, how can we have been receiving the fullness of the Spirit as we ought? How can the evidence of his power be there?

It is the ordinariness, the physical ordinariness, the necessity to use ordinary words, to speak in terms of the ordinary things we are doing, the conversation just like any other conversation —it is this that tends to make us doubt that anything extra-ordinary can be happening. Belief is pushed back into the church building, into discussion for people who 'like that kind of thing'. Ordinary living is left to go its own way, according to prevailing standards and influences. 'Is not this Joseph's son?' has its exact parallel in our difficulty in believing that the Spirit can be at work in one carpenter's shop, in one street, in one home.

A question to the new communicant member such as : 'Do you believe in God as your heavenly Father—do you accept Christ as your Saviour and the Holy Spirit as your guide?' can become as abstract and intellectual as these words 'Repent and believe' seem in the book of 'Acts'. By themselves they can seem to be like expecting a man to say: 'I'm prepared to accept that this may be true'—but adding to himself 'I must make my reservations about what I think is reasonable and possible in the life I myself have to live'.

It is this emphasis on what he has to accept *intellectually*, and the lack of being accepted *as a person*, which the agnostic, the sceptic, the inwardly defeated, sees first, and all too often it turns him away. Something has to convince people *at their own level* before they can want to turn from what they are and what they think and be drawn to this other experience, this exploration which is setting these other people on fire— and from that to go on to see if what happened in the Scriptures, and is declared to be happening now, can happen to them.

We have to accept them, if we are to understand what it means that we are accepted in Christ. 'In a word, accept one another as Christ accepted us, to the glory of God' (Romans, ch. 15, v. 17—N.E.B.).

This is what we read of in 'Acts': Ananias saying 'Brother Saul' to the man who had persecuted the Church and had not had time to enough prove his repentance; Peter accepting Cornelius, accepting the divine correction from one who was not a believer in Peter's sense; the uneducated, the social outcasts, being accepted and discovered to be the channels of God's truth to the apostles who had known and loved and learned of the Lord himself.

This is always the humanly unbelievable—and this is how we have to come to believe, because belief is not a purely human action. The power to believe belongs to the power given us by the Spirit.

If I want men to be different before I will accept them I am renouncing the Gospel. If I wish they would show more desire to be different . . . show shame . . . show more gratitude . . . if I wish they had this and that which they have not got . . . 'then,' I say to myself, 'I could accept them and feel that we belong together.' But my acceptance of them ought to be of the same kind as God's.

Instead, I am often looking for them to repent and believe *before* I can accept them. I am believing what God did for me in Christ, that he accepts me as I am on what Christ has done for me, not on what I have done. Yet I am looking for them justifying themselves before being accepted by me. I am looking for them redeeming themselves, giving themselves a standing from which to be accepted, and I am showing it in the unsuspected moments of my ordinary conduct and conversation, in my attitudes, my looks, the tone of my voice.

We do not repent and believe in order to be accepted. We repent and believe because we have been accepted, because Christ has put us right with God; and the proof of it is in the Resurrection and the Holy Spirit. We repent and believe because God has taken it on himself. 'While we were yet sinners, Christ died for us . . .'; 'not for our sins only but for the sins of the whole world'. We have seen it—and we find it to be true in signs which we cannot doubt. We do not by our faith, our own human faith, become worthy to be accepted.

When I shield myself from real giving and receiving with other men I am demanding of them what God has not required of me—or of them. I am not standing by them on the same level, in the same need. I am a fellow-sinner—but not quite in the same sense. I let myself think I am in a different position because, however inadequately, I do believe I have 'repented and believed the Gospel'; I have 'believed in the Lord Jesus Christ'. But I am turning it, however subtly, to my credit; I am saying to myself that at least I have opened my eyes to see and recognise and give myself over to what I have seen and recognised. But who opened my eyes?

This is what lies behind Paul's words 'preaching' and 'Gospel'. This is how we have to learn to see—by going to others and saying 'Come'. This is how we have to learn to believe—by going to others and saying 'Help us to believe'.

Much of the work of the Holy Spirit must be in secret. 'The wind bloweth where it listeth . . .' And it is true that it is often through other people that we receive what the Spirit is here to give.

This is what we have to learn: where to place ourselves so that we may be in a position to receive, they and we together; how to accept other people in such a way that we are true to our own acceptance in Christ, but also learning what we cannot know without them. They have no answer, any more than we by ourselves have, to the basic problems of the world—violence, individual aggressiveness, greed and suffering.

This receiving must of necessity happen more often outside the walls of the church than within. The technology of our age comes into it, because it creates the ways men think, what they consider life is for, what they seek and what they fear. The sciences are in it, the politics, the restructuring of the world's economy—because this is the stuff of our conversation with men. Their concern for the world and our concern for the world meet here, in the practicalities of the world's life.

7 · We have to be taught with unbelievers

George Matheson, author of the hymn 'O Love that wilt not let me go', says of the feeding of the five thousand that the disciples needed the multitude at that moment more than the multitude needed the disciples. The disciples thought that the crowd's need was for bread; and the crowd's need was for hands which would share bread, for the touch of common humanity, for a 'secular' sharing of bread; and they were right. In the secular need they were seeing more deeply into the ways of God than were the disciples.

The Church is the fellowship of disciples who are trying to find together what the Lord requires of them; but they have to learn alongside men who make no profession of belief. We so often accept what other men do for us, but not *themselves*. We accept such insights as these from all kinds of people, with all kinds of expertise: how healing of mind can come when the mentally ill share in common tasks, how men and women can be helped out of introversion by gaining confidence in conversation with others, how the impulse to anti-social behaviour can be reduced in its compulsive power. (Borstal boys looking after handicapped children in camps and discovering compassion without acknowledging the word; 'children's panels' taking the place of police courts for young offenders.)

There is so much being done in the exploration of the human personality, the causes of fear and tension, the nature of the involvement of person with person; concern for the 'deviant', the deprived, the children of broken homes, the homeless, the hungry, the drop-outs of society, the despairing, the solitary, the people who do not fit into the type of organised community we have created.

Much of this insight has come through men and women who do not accept the Christian faith. And yet their work not only relates to the Christian truth about how human life is constituted, how it goes wrong, how it goes right, but points to deep truths about the relationships of the Kingdom of God which we have neglected or not allowed ourselves to see because they were too demanding and disturbing. Often there has been more disturbance of mind and conscience about the intricacies of the social and political sins of the world outside the fellowship of the Churches than within. We have been 'at ease' when we had no right to be. We have been tolerating when we should have been rebelling ('turning the world upside down'). There has sometimes been more self-sacrificing love in these works of mercy by those who cannot call themselves Christians than we have shown ourselves. And all too often it has been from the ranks of Christians that vindictiveness in punishment has come; revulsion at misconduct with little investigation of its causes; vehemence for war without assessment of the social structures bearing the stamp of men's sin and encouraging motives which Christ condemned; callousness towards the conditions in which the 'labour force' lived who created the common wealth; setting an example of godly living in charity and uprightness but separating ourselves from those whose sins were socially offensive to us.

We have to learn from the people who have these insights and this dedication to share with us; and with the 'drop-outs', the rebels, the disaffected, the nonconformists of society, and the whole range of the young, blindly groping for an 'alternative society', getting 'hooked' on drugs, taking up cults and creeds which seem to offer a way out of the boredom they are living in.

How do we 'accept' them? By being drawn by 'natural' sympathy? Not with all of them—not with the arrogant, not with the ignorant who despise the Christian faith without knowing much about it, not with those who cultivate a pose of freedom and get themselves enslaved by commercial exploiters. To accept these as they are needs what we do not have in ourselves—love like Christ's, patience like his, the power to speak and listen and discern beyond the surface words and attitudes.

We have to be 'free men' to do this—we need freedom from the selves which are in the tension of wrong relationship with God, resulting in wrong relationship with men—and that is what Christ has won for us. This is the work of the Holy Spirit—the enlightening of the eyes of our understanding to know that we are accepted in Christ, and set free to be a new creation in him. It is impossible for us; possible only in him.

These people are part of the new creation. This may seem unbelievable to us. We have to be given the power to believe it, the power to speak, the power to listen, which belongs to the new creation, however unlikely it seems that people like these (and ourselves) can exercise it.

Unless the Holy Spirit is true we have no way of accepting them which takes us farther than tolerance and a measure of understanding and sympathy. We have all the evidence in the pages of the New Testament how the disciples and apostles found it impossible 'with men'—and then a fact 'with God'. 'Forbid him, for he followeth not with us' was a first sign of the impossible. The words which came to their lips were words like 'I have never . . .'. They had to learn. They had to discover the unbelievable. How could these outsiders be brought in, accepted, made to belong, by the words and impulses of ordinary human nature? This had to be act of God, power of God, wisdom of God, love of God. It belonged to his amazing gift in Christ. The people 'outside' were accepted by 'grace'.

This was the proof that the Holy Spirit had sent the believers out. This was the sign of their repentance and faith; and this was what men saw in them before they understood the meaning of it and the source of it. They saw the Cross and the Resurrection without at first knowing it. They saw a love which received them astonishingly, without knowledge at first that this was nothing less than the love of God in its fullness, 'poured out' on men. They saw it in the way they were received, in the way they were listened to, in the way these Christians were prepared to sit with them and learn from them as well as with them. They saw it in the freedom the Christians had in speaking to them. They saw it even before the Christians had told what had happened to them, before the testimony, before the evidence, before the acclamation of what God had done in Christ—and therefore before the teaching, before the doctrine, before the claim that this was Gospel and the way of salvation.

The supernatural was there before it was called supernatural —in that very kind of receiving which was 'out of this world'. These people 'outside' did not know the word 'grace'—but they recognised a new dimension of love. They did not know what it meant that Christ had made atonement for the sins of the world, that reconciliation had come between sinful man and holy God, that Christ had 'made peace' and destroyed the enmity. These things had to be explained. The words and the work of Christ had to be interpreted. But the fact and the nature of their acceptance by those who called themselves Christians was the first evidence of these mysteries— the proof of what God had done in Christ, although they did not yet know it was that. Their being accepted belonged with the 'acceptance in the beloved', the divine mystery of Calvary.

This is no 'cheap grace'. It begins and continues in the simplest things, in the look in the eyes which anyone can understand; but what is uncovered, gradually or suddenly, is the depth, height, length and breadth of the love of God. Human sin becomes more terrible, because it is a continuing denial, defiance of a God who has accepted us for what Christ is and has done for us. It is refusal to accept being accepted— refusal to see the cost of being accepted, the need to be accepted. It makes the Cross unnecessary.

And yet our acceptance of being accepted is simple; and so also must be the acceptance which other men take from us, knowing it for what it is without first of all analysing and assessing it. 'By this shall all men know that ye are my disciples . . .' All men.

Faith that we have been accepted in Christ 'while we are yet sinners' is inseparable from accepting our brother in the faith that Christ needs him. We are incomplete without him. Christ is incomplete without him. In accepting him we are 'making up what is lacking in the sufferings of Christ'. We are brothers in learning one another's need. Our brother, our neighbour, is the man to whom the Holy Spirit sends us to learn of Christ and be empowered to do 'greater works than these'.

Men must be received, not just to be told their deficiencies in belief, but because they are part of the world for which Christ died; they are themselves this world, this redeemed humanity, still awaiting the revelation of what has happened to it.

The kind of grace needed for it? Willingness to receive them against the pull of prejudices, our fear of what this will do to the Church; our apprehensiveness about what they may do to our faith; readiness to give up what is shown to be a hindrance to the Gospel, readiness to re-shape the familiar habits of our congregations, to welcome new knowledge even when it is disturbing, to learn where the strains and stresses of the world's work are, to be patient with the casualties of a society which has little incentive towards the Gospel values, to encourage the rebellious young to open their minds without embarrassment, to give time to the eccentric who cannot conform to the life of the world and does not know that it has been judged and superseded—readiness to do what we have never done before, to be to strangers what we have never thought it necessary to be, to be with the kind of people we have been accustomed to leave to go their own way. This is where the Gospel is first seen—in us. This is freedom from our inhibitions, our human-nature reactions, our prejudices, our own built-in personalities.

To receive the Spirit immediately and also through other people is the same as saying, as Jesus did, that to enter into God's forgiveness we must forgive; to humble ourselves under the mighty hand of God we must be 'clothed with humility one toward another'; and to submit ourselves to God we must be willing to submit ourselves to one another.

It is not a case of receiving the Spirit and going out to find the implications. We have to be 'out' as well as 'in' in order to receive the Holy Spirit at all. We have to be with our brothers outside, even with our enemy, standing by them in equal need, in order to receive. There is no 'in-church', where the Holy Spirit dwells exclusively ('he dwelleth not in temples made with hands') and an 'outside' where we take him. He is already 'outside', where the doubter is; and doubt is for many of us the other side of faith. He is where the man in prison is, and we are all transgressors. He is where the stranger is; and we are all, in some of our neediest moments, strangers. He is where the sick are—and we are all sick men whom God has to make whole. He is where the hungry are; and we are all dependent on others for the necessaries of life, so he is where men are struggling to find how the hungry of the world are to be fed. He has a mind about how it is to be done. He has a mind about how the trade of the world is to be carried on, how enemy nations are to become neighbour nations. He is there 'outside' where the search is on, where the revolt is on against any system which stimulates the false motives and sees the motives of the kingdom of God as impracticable.

We have to be there if we are to receive the fullness of the Spirit, the power of the Spirit—out there as well as 'inside' where we lift up our hearts in believing prayer, in gladness and obedience; out there where we fight the good fight of faith and learn our own need alongside the need of our brother, and the total need of our world—praying out there in our hearts if not on our lips because we are crying out from the common sin and need of men, as well as praying inside the fellowship in the 'stillness where our spirits walk', to hear the still small voice for intimate correction, rebuke, guidance and love.

So often we think we can be broken into by that power of

the Spirit, without exposing ourselves where the Spirit is at work to save the world. The more inevitable the present life of the world seems, the more urgent is that work of the Spirit, and the more urgent is the need for us to be there.

But are our congregations functioning like that, shaped and directed for that? Is it out there that we see the humanitarian impulses and rightly take them as evidences of the presence of God? Is it out there we learn how much more there is in God than we have yet experienced?

God in the 'secular' affairs of life—our generation has been true to many of these insights, correcting the idea that God is chiefly to be discovered in church and in a refined spirituality which has then somehow to 'express itself' in the ordinary work of life. The corrective is right; it is in the work of the world that we have to learn to see God—not just in worship and in 'being apart', not just in solitariness but also where man has to work and think and decide with man.

The new dimension from the Spirit is to be discovered out there. It is a new dimension. It is miracle. It is 'grace'. The Holy Spirit means 'power from on high', wisdom not our own, the interfusing of life and life at depth, beyond psychological insight and adjustment—all of it 'out there'.

If there is nothing corresponding to the powers released in the happenings in 'Acts' we have come right out of the Scriptural experiences and are using Scriptural words for what is no longer recognisable as Scripture. The 'good news' no longer means for us what it means there. The freedom of the Christian comes to mean freedom from enslavement to certain moral faults; it is not the Gospel freedom of being released into the relationship to God and man which Christ opened up for us— the 'new and living way into holiness'. To talk about the 'liberty wherewith Christ has made us free' has lost its meaning.

In Scripture it does not mean a development of our sympathies and capacities but a liberation into the very life of Christ and the capacity to learn to love as he loves. We are baptised by the Spirit to do specific Christ-like works.

If there is no fullness of God, no power of the Spirit, in the 'secular' world of our day the Gospel is not good news for the whole life of men. If there is no supernatural miracle of grace to be received there, no reconciliation (God to man, man to man), there is no Gospel of new life for the day-to-day lives of men. It may well be true that the power of the Spirit showed itself in the apostolic age in some forms which were for that time alone, a specific empowering for the specific beginnings, as on the day of Pentecost; but our inclination is to write off the power itself, the empowering for the conflict with the principalities and powers and the evil motivation in men and society which is still a power of darkness, all the more insidious because of its sophistication and acceptability as the way of life for the technological age.

God overcomes the world through the work-talk of the craftsman, through the slang-talk of the young, through the jargon talk of the specialist, through the philosophising talk of the cynic and the despairing—not only through spiritual language. (How are the words 'Repent' and 'Believe' to be translated for them—how else than by the facts compelling them to find their own words for it?)

My acceptance of people is not only the test of my belief; it is part of my belief. I am giving thanks out of their lives as well as out of my own; I am praying as from them, and sharing in Christ's intercession. Worship outside the walls and worship inside the walls meets here. Without our readiness to be where God wants us to be, to speak where other men speak, to learn along with them what we all need to know, to pray for those who do not yet pray, to be where we can learn to love, where we can learn to repent, where we can learn to believe in what God can do—without that we are not truly asking for the Holy Spirit. We are not ready to be given the power to do the works of Christ.

8 · Not far from the Kingdom

It is somewhere here, in lack of readiness, in lack of expectancy, in unwillingness to believe that the men who work in the ordinary things of the world's life are to be the means of the Church's receiving of the Spirit, that the Gospel is most easily lost. The word 'supernatural' drops out because we do not believe that God has anything directly to do with the natural.

It is precisely here that the supreme discovery has to be made whether God, as he is revealed to us in the Gospel records, is or is not; whether his action amongst men is recognisable and receivable or not. It happens here; or it does not happen. The phenomena of it, even when distorted in the Churches by contradictory or mistaken interpretation and by rash human dogmatism, are either here or not—and if here, to be explored and experienced in the full Gospel sense, or confined to the recognisable areas of psychology.

This is the ultimate question. Is there the immediate, realistic relationship between God and man which justifies the words 'the amazing gift of love', interpreted by other Bible words like 'grace', the more difficult 'justification' (being brought into immediate relationship with God by what Christ has done for us) and 'sanctification' (being given the power to become Christ-like)? If not, the word 'Gospel' is not 'Gospel' in the New Testament sense. Our 'good news' is not the good news which set the apostles on fire. There is no miraculous new life springing from the death and resurrection of Jesus. There is nothing remotely related to a 'redemption' from sin (nor, in fact, sin), no kingdom of heaven as Jesus believed in it, no eternal life for those whom God has taken to himself into that intimate relationship of love, no decisiveness about our willingness to be taken up into it and therefore no rejection and no judgment in the Cross for us—no clear difference between those who believe and those who do not. There is no dimension which needs the word 'supernatural', no wisdom beyond ourselves. Above all, there is nothing that we can call love in us towards God. We can have no delight in what he is, no joy, as Christ knew it—part of his legacy to us. None of this can be, if there are only human personal forces at work. We have no right to use these Gospel words for anything less than the intimacy of personal love, between God and ourselves.

It is at this very point, where we imply the 'values' of God in human life—the caring, the compassion, the concern for the suffering, the passion for justice, the ineradicable belief that a supportive and stimulating kind of society should be possible for men—it is just here that we are tempted to systematise it all into a philosophy of human action, our own estimate of the good and the possible, and to close our minds against the spiritual logic of these signs: that they point farther—to caring, compassion, justice, community in relationship between God and men—in fact, to the Gospel, to the high seriousness of how we stand with God, what he requires of us, what he has done for us; all that is meant by the work of Christ revealed to us by the Holy Spirit.

When we fall into this temptation we distort the Gospel; we eliminate from our thinking the miracle of God's mercy and the miracle of the new life in Christ. We turn the Gospel into something which sums up human endeavour, something man-discovered and man-limited.

Today, when creation is being laid open to us in dramatic power, and unthought-of potentialities are being uncovered in mankind, we are under immense pressure to re-state the Gospel of the love of God in the terms these sciences give us and to relegate its demands to the realm of human ideals and endeavour; and it becomes obsolete in the form in which it is given us in Scripture; and we can gradually and almost imperceptibly become a church, a congregation, without Gospel, a church tied (not free), a church with a worship, a liturgy, proclaiming 'mighty acts of God' which do not any longer happen, using language in prayer which is such an exaggeration of what we expect as to be almost hypocritical.

The old words, the Biblical words, the basic Biblical belief about the meaning of the death of Christ, what happened between God and man because of the Cross—all this remains in our Communion services: 'Lamb of God, that takest away the sins of the world'; 'Send down the Holy Spirit to sanctify both us and these thine own gifts of bread and wine, that the bread which we break may be to us the communion of the body of Christ and the cup which we bless the communion of the blood of Christ'. Here, however we modernise the words and re-interpret, is reconciliation through the Cross, salvation, the power of the Holy Spirit, the grace of the Lord Jesus Christ. Here, if words mean anything, is the miracle of the immediacy of God and the empowering of all who repent and believe . . . the 'new covenant in the blood of Christ'. (The Churches with obligatory liturgy have the merit or the embarrassment of retaining more strictly the Biblical words and doctrine; the other Churches may 'adapt' and create what may seem no more than a 'remembrance day' service for Christ.)

Here it is, whatever our denomination, set down at the heart of our worship. But is it basic to the belief and action of the congregation? Is it basic to preaching—that 'one died for all', that we are redeemed by his sacrifice, whatever interpretation we may give of the Cross; that he has made atonement for our sins; that he is the 'propitiation for our sins and not for our sins only but for the sins of the whole world'? However we re-interpret, however we change the language for contemporary understanding, the fact of a new relationship between God and man is claimed by the Scriptures to be the Gospel and is basic to the Holy Communion. This alone is what brings 'glory', the shout of joy, triumph, exultation, into Christian worship.

There must be bewilderment often between what the congregations hear said at such times and what it is in fact doing (and believing); between the action of the Sacrament, the miracle of grace implicit in it, and the action to which we are only exhorted, the action which is still our own effort, our own endeavour to live the life commanded.

'How do you receive the Spirit?' becomes the sharpest of words. Is it by seeing good, seeing compassion, learning sensitiveness, discovering relationship, having concern for the deprived and anger against exploitation—seeing this and holding to it because, if this is good, this is God? Is this how the Spirit is received, this way and no other?

What, in fact, is our equivalent for 'repent and believe', standing with our generation in sin and perplexity and insight, and learning with them what these words mean today? Not just another way of 'communicating' words but a contemporary way of learning and acting on what this means? Repent, turn—from what to what? From what attitude to other people? From what attitude to society, to politics, to economic developments, to individual ambition—to God? And by what power? Our own—or is there a power of the Spirit for this? And to believe in what, instead? What kind of relationships, what kind of learning how to live along with other people, what kind of freedom, what kind of release into new 'openness'? What potentialities, capacities, to be drawn out beneath the surface level of our opinions and judgments? Belief in what kind of God?

'Believe?' To have expectancy that a different kind of life is possible for individuals and society? That this cannot be comprehended within our usual processes of reasoning—that it must be a different kind of reasoning; that it must be 'the mind of Christ'? By what power? Our own—or is there a power of the Spirit? These are the fundamental questions.

Many of this generation seem to be poised between a searching which is honest, discerning, even sacrificial, and belief which causes them great difficulty in the form given in Scripture, because it does not seem to have any meaning for them. 'Multitudes in the valley of decision', having to live in the world as it is, in the 'rat race', determined to reject many of its values and most of its bland assumptions about the motives and objectives proper for men and the accepted limits of human experience—but seeing no alternative; and yet many of them receiving a kind of power, a new insight, what is even being called dedication, 'spirituality', when they commit themselves to this search, this rejection of current values, this obstinate or angry conviction that there must be a better life for men. But what measure of power? The 'fullness of God'? The 'baptism' to do the works of Christ?

That must come from the belief that what they are seeking *has happened*; what all of us are meant to be, one man *has been* —the turning, the repenting, done completely by him. This is belief *vindicated*, while we by ourselves are still mainly arguing about it.

Many are poised today where they will have to act on belief as it is given us in 'Acts', however strange the words; on that central fact of Jesus—not just their own selections of his teaching and their homage to his sacrifice but the whole Jesus Christ, and all that happened because of him. Having gone so far to understand him and believe in what he was and is, they will have to do more simply what he told us to do, what the Church of the apostles did—ask as the first Christians did, ask that all he won, all that burst out in power in his death and resurrection, all that was in him, be given us—ask and by asking lay ourselves open to receive it. 'When you ask, believe that you have received . . .' Believe in Christ in that sense—believe he is alive, believe he is here, believe we can speak to him, believe we can trust him, and that he is able to do for us 'far above all that we can ask or think'.

It is typical of our generation to question whether we need the immediate action of God to give us the Spirit precisely because we are always living by benefit of the Spirit, always sharing in what has come to men through the Spirit. In this way we are gradually edged away towards thinking that this is all that the receiving of the Spirit means.

What more is this power? How do we find out? Still, as always, by two kinds of action: by that asking; and by that standing with our brother which is the first practical step to learning to love him.

This means being with some who cannot use the Bible words, with some who say they cannot believe as we do, cannot pray, cannot be sure that what is recorded as having happened in the beginning is a clear directive for us today. It means accepting them in the position they are in, understanding it, sharing with them in it, making ourselves one with them in it.

We are set our most difficult questions here—questions we are often evading. How far can we work together with those who do not share our beliefs, who have a different view of human nature?

The issues can perhaps be seen most clearly in our co-operation as Christians with the psychiatrists and psychologists; whether or not they are Christians. There is the level where neurosis is diagnosed and medically treated—the level of medical expertise. There is the exposure of tension. There is the burden of guilt in some area of relationship which is the cause of alternating outburst and contrition. That points to an area of co-operation, for the uncovering of it is a work of compassion we can share in and learn from. There may be treatment for 'adjustment' between husband and wife, or parents and child, which involves an understanding of how the maladjustment has come about, the cause of fear or resentment. That points to something from which we can certainly learn. But if the Gospel is true, if the depth of human relationship involves God, involves who Christ is, involves the power of the 'Spirit', the final work is not in the hands of the psychiatrist or minister. The final work is love—and God's love, not ours. Adjustment is not enough. Relationship must be learned by relationship—and for the Christian the relationship impossible for men is possible with God.

This is the kind of exploration we have to do if we are to stand with our brother the psychiatrist in faith, to learn and to be used for the opening of new dimensions.

We can see the issues pin-pointed quite simply in radio and television programmes: for example, 'Have you a problem?' Many of these problems involve intricately difficult breakdown of relationship between husband and wife, parents and children. The Christian would not think of approaching these problems without prayer; he believes that in these depths only God can heal and give new life. Is this prayer effectual? If it is, the answers given to problems at that depth without any reference to prayer are not effectual. Yet there can be other levels of problem where the insight has the true mark of Christian wisdom and understanding. How can we learn new dimensions unless we learn together? But the impression left by these programmes, if they are not in any Christian context or shared in by Christians, is that these problems, basic to human nature, can and must be worked out by us 'on our own', without any reference to a 'supernatural' God. Christian belief is set aside as irrelevant or positively misleading.

The whole area of social welfare abounds in 'cases' where there is no easy answer; and we can be wrong in so many ways and right in so many ways.

The preaching of the Gospel was for Paul part of the proof of the miracle of Christ because, when truly evidenced, it had the same power as Christ's, not the wisdom of men but the wisdom of God working in men what they could not work in themselves, so that the preaching was itself the proof of the Gospel. This preaching today has to take many forms, and one of them is being where the needs of men, their total needs, are being uncovered, and the 'caring callings' are at work. But this does not mean handing over to them, giving up the belief which they need in the same degree as we do.

The Spirit seems something 'not for us' only when thought of as confined within the language and liturgy of the Church.

When the Spirit is received in the work of the world and is seen to be about the work of the world, the strains and tensions, the joy of right living, it is ordinary words we speak and hear, ordinary situations we are told about, ordinary problems, carried to a new dimension, lifted up into the mind of Christ but not away from the experience we all know: the cup of cold water, the taking in of the stranger, the visiting of the sick, the feeding of the hungry.

In the ordinary things—for we receive the Spirit where we are under severest pressure to deny him, to conform to the prevailing thought, to be impressed by human cleverness, to wish to be worldly-wise. We receive simplicity at the point of the world's sophistication where we are pulled into argument at the world's level, humility at the point where we are in the toils of the world's philosophic pride, the power to love where we are often likely to be at difference with other people—in fact just where we have been told that without Christ we can do none of these things.

We have to be open to correction, prepared to be patient under rebuke, 'enduring the contradiction of sinners', ready to learn some truth from those who do not seem to us to have any particular right to teach us.

This is part of what it means to accept people as we believe ourselves to be accepted of God, to be humbled to know we are no better than they and yet to be believing in that miracle which is for them as well as for ourselves, to be asking for it, to be expectant of it, to be praying that our words may carry a power which is not (to us) in them, to be a faith for those who have not found faith.

This is the test of the preaching of the people of God. The very point where we are tempted to doubt the power is the point where the Spirit is to be received.

Over and above those with whom we work every day, where do we meet with those outside who do not share our belief? We must go to them. Few of them will come to us. The church notice-board will not bring them in. Special meetings in the church hall still imply that they are to come in to learn to be like us—and God is working for something better than that.

We have done little in exploration of this—places outside the congregation where we can meet with those who are responsible for the whole community's life—local government, social work, political associations, executive and unions in industry, the educational units, the places where the community's public opinion is formed, where men form their convictions about what life is for.

We may have our unity of fellowship within the congregation, for prayer, for service, for the opening up of the Scriptures. We have the congregational unit itself—in sacrament, in worship, in preaching, in mission. The Spirit is there. But we cannot receive the Spirit solely within the walls. Much in our church buildings and organisations would suggest we can. The book of 'Acts' clearly says we cannot.

Here is a fundamental need—as fundamental as the receiving of the Sacraments and the prayer of the small group; for this is placing the total work of God in the world in the one context, looking for his mercy and grace for the whole of life. This is 'mission', without which we do not receive the power of the Spirit, for the Spirit is received for the whole work of Christ, that he may see of the travail of his soul and be satisfied. We are baptised in the Spirit for this work.

9 · The Church—in fear and in faith

We are in the Galatian situation today in our temptation to pull ourselves back into concentration on the practices of the Faith, to set down rigidly what is to be observed in order to satisfy God, what is to be our means of proving ourselves in God's sight, putting ourselves right with him, fulfilling our duty to the Church and making ourselves worthy to be called by Christ's name.

Paul's question is for us, as it was for the Judaizers in Galatia. This is a bondage—and there are increasing signs of it. We are being tempted to call men back, away from the faith and freedom of the Gospel, into observance of good acts. We are calling for support of the Church, service to the Church, maintenance of the Church, witness to moral standards— instead of first of all and fundamentally and passionately, to the 'free gift of God', the mercy and new life, the glorious liberty of the children of God—the miracle of being accepted, the miracle of being empowered ('sanctified'), the miracle of being promised that the kingdom of heaven is laid open to us, that we shall be 'like Christ'.

This is a deep and subtle temptation. It seems self-evident

71

that the Church must be maintained and upheld. It seems unanswerable that in a time of permissiveness the Christian standards of conduct must be safeguarded. And yet we can work ourselves into a position where, in defending Gospel and Church, we are closing our minds to the Gospel as the miracle of God's saving act for all men and to the Holy Spirit as his immediate giving to all who will receive.

This defensiveness can take many forms, as we saw earlier. It can be a defence of the faith as expressed in the confessional statements of former generations, a rear-guard action for the very form of words by which the Gospel was preached and the Church established in other days, and an insistence that it must be through these words, through these practices, that men must come to Christ. And this can become like the bondage of the first Jewish Christians in being driven back to the rigid observance of the Law. In spite of its language of faith it can come to mean a concentration on what men must do to show faith, to justify themselves.

Or, at the other extreme, it can be a defence of the Churches as they are, the organisations as we have become accustomed to them with their undeniable good works, service of the needy along the channels which are now traditional, 'mission' in the form of energetic endeavours to reach people outside the Church and show them the value of belonging to it, worship in the form familiar to us, with all its associations with what has been best in our lives, and preaching which recalls us to 'whatsoever things are true . . . honest . . . of good report', so that we can think of them and get the other things into perspective.

All of it good—but can it stand up to Paul's question and the searching Scripture in it? What is at the centre of it all? What is it that we are trying to do for men? Is that, in fact, what it is: what we are *trying* to do for men and for ourselves —something *we* do to receive God's blessing and help? Or is it the Gospel of the love of God, the love beyond the power of men, beyond their worthiness, beyond their capacity—which is the gift of God in Christ, the free gift, the 'grace'?

Preaching can be arresting and helpful; the work of the Church can be worthy of support; the worship can turn our thoughts to God; and yet it can all get the emphasis ultimately wrong and become only an exhortation to our activity, our thinking, our rectitude, our measure of human kindness, our own 'law of love', instead of to the work of Christ for us and in us which, received and obeyed, becomes a new dimension of love, new thinking, new impulses, new horizons, new standards, new freedom.

Paul's question to the Jewish Christians is as sharply pointed for Christians and Christian congregations today. What is at the heart of it all? What kind of faith? 'How have you received the Spirit?'

We can be wrong about this in the same two ways. We can be wrong if we are only endeavouring to learn from the enlightened humanism of our times. We can be wrong if we are only thinking how we can save the Church.

It is given us by our Lord himself how the world is to be saved, by what power, by what human agencies of the power of God; what it means today to be 'fishers of men' like the first disciples; what it means to be told 'As the Father hath sent me, so send I you'; and why 'greater things than these shall he do'.

What have we today as the equivalent of the places where Jesus himself and the Church and the apostles encountered the life of the world for its saving—the courts of the Temple where the thinkers of the day were in debate; the market-place where men could ask 'What has this to do with our buying and selling?'; the forum where public opinion was formed by the public figures of community and state, the local court where Roman justice was having to ask what the 'good' was; the work-place where Paul plied his trade with others; the harbour where fishermen philosophised—all those places where men could congregate to hear and be moved to see the meaning of this new life—or be roused to defend themselves? Have we got our minds so firmly fixed on church buildings and meetings, and bringing people into them, that we can scarcely think how a congregation might be functioning anywhere else? The Church has always been 'sent out'—it sometimes had to be the church meeting on the hill-side, the church meeting in the house, or the church meeting by the riverside on the stance of another sect. It may for us have to be, in part, in our buildings —but what kind of buildings, for what purposes? And it may have to be, far more than we have yet seen, outside the walls, where the fundamental questions are put to us, who we are and what we stand for—questions put by what other men are and not only by their words.

Most fundamental of all, the question coming straight from their own living; what have we to declare of the 'wonderful works of God?' What is our equivalent today for 'They brought to him all sick people who were taken with divers diseases and torments and those who were lunatic . . .?' Is it that they are now taken to hospital, or that the doctor calls, and that this is how the healing work of Jesus is now carried on? All of it? Was that all Jesus gave them in his healing? Should they not also be brought before the congregation for prayer in the power of the Holy Spirit? Do we pass the whole of the healing to the medical profession, the whole of the social work to its whole-time servants, the whole of the ordering of the community's life to the expertise of those who stand to gain most from it?

How are we to make the Church of Jesus Christ, doing his work, a Church which can say the equivalent of 'Go and tell John the things which ye have seen and heard'? What, in hard fact, is happening which can be explained only in the New Testament way, as the signs of something which is beyond human powers and yet is being accomplished through ordinary men and women?

We make it hard for men to believe today when we cannot say these words, when there is no evidence that we are adding a new power to healing, finding the motives of the Kingdom in economic struggle for the world's poor, bringing the zest of new life where there is only existence, liberty where there is twisted and perverted personality—if people look today and see almost nothing which would suggest what the Scriptures record and promise, and hear us only exhorting them with ideals which they know well enough already; when they see us tied to the past, enclosed in our customs, in bondage to the institutional shape of the church while we speak and read of a life of 'glorious liberty'?

What the book of 'Acts' shows us is men and women being prayed into the Church, and the Church being prayed out into the places where the decisions of men's lives were taken.

It needed the power of the Holy Spirit to send them out. It needed the power of the Spirit to bring men in. To take the outsider into their company was an act of faith and hope and love on the part of the first Christians of the same order of miracle as their own receiving of the Spirit. It was a freedom which demonstrated the miracle of the freedom of the Gospel. The power was the same kind of power which Jesus had.

The Lord added to the Church. That was how it was. *They* 'continued steadfast in prayer'. That was the dimension in which it was done. It was no notice-board with a welcome on it and a full-time minister to call on those who had recently come into the district. And if it was through one man, as with Barnabas, he was 'full of the Holy Ghost and faith; and much people was added to the Lord'. And if it was one man, Peter, going out, it was often going where he had no wish to go. He was made free to go by the Spirit, against his own inclinations.

Just as I, as a person, need to see my conversation, my meeting with people, my transactions, my agreement, my differences, as the area where I need God and need to learn to do the new things he is requiring of me—in the same kind of way the church, the congregation, is under the same need to be 'set free' to do the new things he is requiring.

There is too much which we think we know quite well how to do; and our minds become rutted in our habits. The idea of a new type of congregation, functioning in a new way, seems out of the question. We become static, enclosed, hardened against the Spirit.

What is involved in a new kind of congregation today? Receiving a man into fellowship unconditionally, not for membership of an organisation but to 'belong' because he is wanted, because he is needed as himself, without any pressures, without any obligations—just to come and see, to give what he has that we may lack—this is what is involved; and it has to be the work of the Lord. Like the apostolic Church, and in some circumstances basically not so very differently, we have to pray this world of violence and confusion, of new knowledge and promise, into the Church—not just to make the Church bigger in a day when its membership is declining;

not first of all to try to convince the agnostics and atheists among them, but in the first instance to make ready to be one new body, a new Church. And the beginning may be to pray ourselves *out* of our buildings into the hot centres of the world.

We shall have special need to hear our Lord's word 'Watch' as men come to be one with us, or we go to be one with them— the technician who does not see beyond his technique, the psychiatrist and the biologist who think that they are getting all the life-force analysed, taped and manipulated. It may shake faith. It may make the Gospel seem more and more remote from 'realities'. And when we are exerting ourselves to see their life and work through their eyes, we may be tempted to eliminate all the elements which to them are obscurantist, mythical, allegorical, before we realise it— becoming, in Paul's word, intellectually 'ashamed' of the Gospel of Christ, ready to discard what does not seem to come within the recognisable accepted categories of contemporary thought.

There is something more than an ordinarily vicious circle at work here. We begin, reasonably enough, with business and industry as concerned with 'things' and with people in their dealings with these 'things', with the relationships involved, with efficiency, profit and reward—and in politics with the 'art of the possible', assuming that we know what is possible in human nature. We go on to see the whole ordering of the world's life—its trade, its economics—in these terms. Then we come back to the 'art of the possible' in our own immediate situation, reinforced in our attitude that God has nothing directly to say about these practicalities, except that there are certain accepted standards of honesty and fair-dealing which decent people observe.

And where do we end up? By assuming that God has

nothing to do with the technicalities of how his children are to be fed, housed, given work to do which teaches a common life; how the resources of the earth are to be shared; how trade is to be developed so that the success of one nation does not involve disaster in another and a war for markets; how economic growth is to be achieved without the inflaming of the very impulses which Christ has judged and condemned. We end up as if nothing of this matters to him because it is not 'spiritual'. And then we are exhorted to have faith. 'Repent! Believe!' The Gospel is argued out of the realities of the world's life and the physical life God has ordained for men on this earth—out into a hazy belief that, whatever happens in war, hunger, suffering, degradation, 'love' is what matters most, whatever 'love' is. 'God cares.' But this love of God does not seem to have encounter with the realities of human life. It has had no victory, except in the sense that we believe that love is better than hate and sacrifice than self-regard. We have no real hope. We cannot look forward with assurance to any fulfilled purpose. Nothing has happened which declares unmistakably the triumph of the love of God over the evil in men. So the Gospel does not relate to what is actually happening in the factories, offices, fields—to Government, to executive offices and trade union meetings. Nothing happens which brings the power of God there.

The Gospel is lost—the Gospel as we are given it in the New Testament. What is the use of the forgiveness of the Cross without the power, the freedom, to live the new life by faith, the 'redeemed' life, which is the gift of God by the Spirit? ('The life which I now live I live by the faith of the Son of God, who loved me and gave himself for me.') And what becomes of the Gospel promises if we cannot begin to live this life now, in the realities which all men have to face?

If we are not 'free' to live a new life, to be a new human nature, how can we talk of 'glorious liberty' now?

The Gospel which is lost is the Gospel which declares that the whole world, the total activity of men, was redeemed by the Cross, that Christ died for the world and not only for individuals adding up one by one to the whole world, died for the saving of the worldly activity of men, died for the common life of men which is to be a preparation for the life of the kingdom of heaven; and that the Holy Spirit is given, therefore, for this very life—so that alienation from God is to be changed into life according to his purposes.

This is to be God's workmanship. Where sin abounds and has elaborated until men can see no way other than the way things have become, there grace must much more abound—in these relationships, in all their complexity, in all their apparent inevitability. And the power of the Spirit is given to work this work.

St Paul's question: Do we believe because of the good we see in the world—or by this Gospel? There is the strongest temptation today for Christians to be two kinds of men; to keep the Gospel of grace for the more intimate of personal relationships and for the fellowship of believing people; and work our way in other matters as other men do, as if the Holy Spirit had not been given, as if Christ had not given us new life for the whole world.

That question—how do we receive the Spirit?—was it only Paul's warning to a few people in a local situation a long time ago in a small Roman province? Or is it for all of us, 'Scripture' for us today?

How else are we to read the signs of our times—not only the decline in power in many places within the Church, the lack of congregational prayer and the New Testament motive of mission; not only the agnosticism of our generation but also the evidence that what should be happening within the Church is happening in tentative and often misunderstood forms outside it, or at least outside the institutional organisations of it: groups of people gathering in houses, in the example of previous generations back to the apostles, for prayer and the opening up of the Scriptures and the discovery of the 'fellowship in the Gospel' and the gift of the Spirit—and young people seeking together in what may seem strange ways and finding a power sometimes strangely like the apostles?

Is the freedom which the Gospel brings being sought and sometimes found outside a hide-bound Church? Is God raising up faith outside the walls? Is he turning, as he has had to do many times, from the Church as an institution to whoever is willing to 'rise up and follow'?